THE CHAMP IS HERE
EL CAMPEÓN ESTA AQUÍ

ACKNOWLEDGEMENT

I Would Like To Acknowledge The CREATOR OF HEAVEN AND EARTH (GOD) FOR ALL THAT HE HAS Given Me. Thanking God I Am For My Talents and Gifts.

I Recognize That The Lord Gave Me This Gift, Which Allows Me To Share With Children And Everyone That Participates In The Reading Of The Literary Material That I Produce Through The Commission Of God.

Thank You Lord God

I Will Forever Be Grateful For Your Trust In Me

Pamela Denise Brown
Goodwill Ambassador
For The Positive Cultivation Of Children

My Collection Of EDUCATIONAL Books are designed to foster the social development of children psychologically. My books are designed to help children become psychologically sociable, culturally sensitive and aware so children can co-exist in diversity and become successful in life. I believe the books I write will transform the minds of children, which ultimately will cause them to pause, to think and make better choices.

My EDUCATIONAL Books are designed to effectuate change and influence success in the lives of every child.

The Smart Books in the Collection are Reinforcements to Learning.

My EDUCATIONAL books will help build children's self-esteem and confidence to a level that will help them socially engage in a diverse world with confidence and harmony and ultimately prepare them for life

Copyright © 2017 Pamela Denise Brown.

All rights reserved. No part of this book may be used or reproduced by any means, graphic, electronic, or mechanical, including photocopying, recording, taping or by any information storage retrieval system without the written permission of the publisher except in the case of brief quotations embodied in critical articles and reviews.

Books Speak For You books may be ordered through booksellers or by contacting:
Booksspeakforyou.com
The views expressed in this work are solely those of the author.
Any illustration provided by iStock and such images are being used for illustrative purposes.
Certain stock imagery © iStock.
Illustrated By: Pamela Denise Brown
ISBN: 978-1-64050-314-4
Library of Congress Control Number: 2017908455
Printed in the United States Of America

A Champion Is A Person Who Has Defeated Or Surpassed All Rivals In A Competition.

A Champion Is A Winner, A Record Holder, A Person That Succeeds.

A Champion Is Number One, A King, A Prize Winner, A Victor.

A Champion Is A Person That's Undefeated, Unbeaten.

A Champion Is Someone That's The Greatest, Someone That's On Top, Someone That's Topnotch And Outstanding!!!

The Champ Is Here

Be The Champion In Your Life!!!

The "Champ" Is Here

I
Fight

PELEO (Spanish)

How Do You Fight?
¿Cómo peleas? (Spanish)

_____

_____

_____

_____

I Win

Yo Ganar (Spanish)

How Do You Win?
¿Cómo se gana? (Spanish)

_____
_____
_____
_____

I
Battle

Yo batalla (Spanish)

How Do You Battle?
¿Cómo batallas? (Spanish)

_____
_____
_____
_____

I Compete

Yo compito (Spanish)

How Do You Compete?
¿Cómo compites? (Spanish)

_____
_____
_____
_____

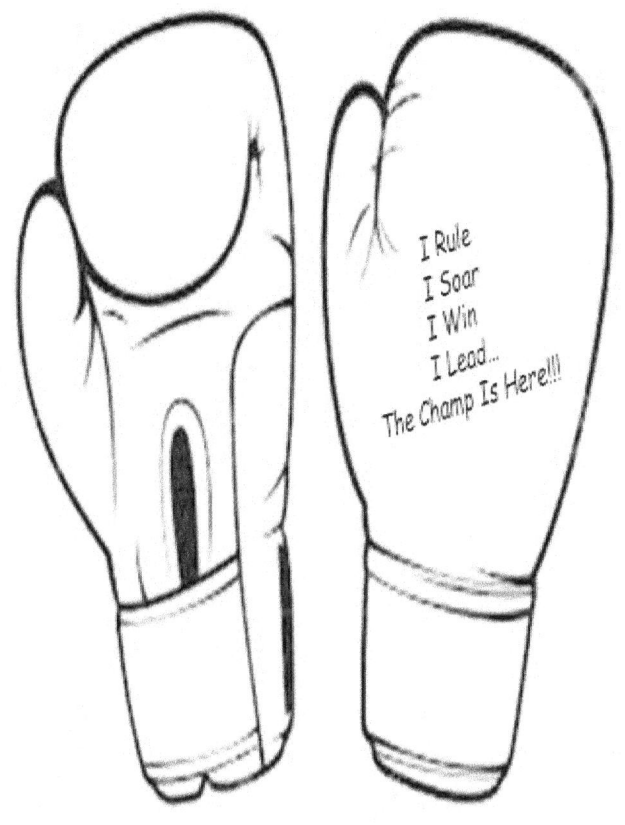

color the gloves in your champion color

I
Slay

Yo mato (Spanish)

How Do You Slay?
¿Cómo matas? (Spanish)

_____

_____

_____

_____

_____

I Conquer

Yo conquisto (Spanish)

How Do You Conquer?
Cómo conquistar (Spanish)

_____
_____
_____
_____
_____

I Endure

Yo aguanto (Spanish)

How Do You Endure?
¿Cómo aguantas? (Spanish)

_____
_____
_____
_____

I
Excel

Yo Excel (Spanish)

How Do You Excel?
¿Cómo sobresale? (Spanish)

_____

_____

_____

_____

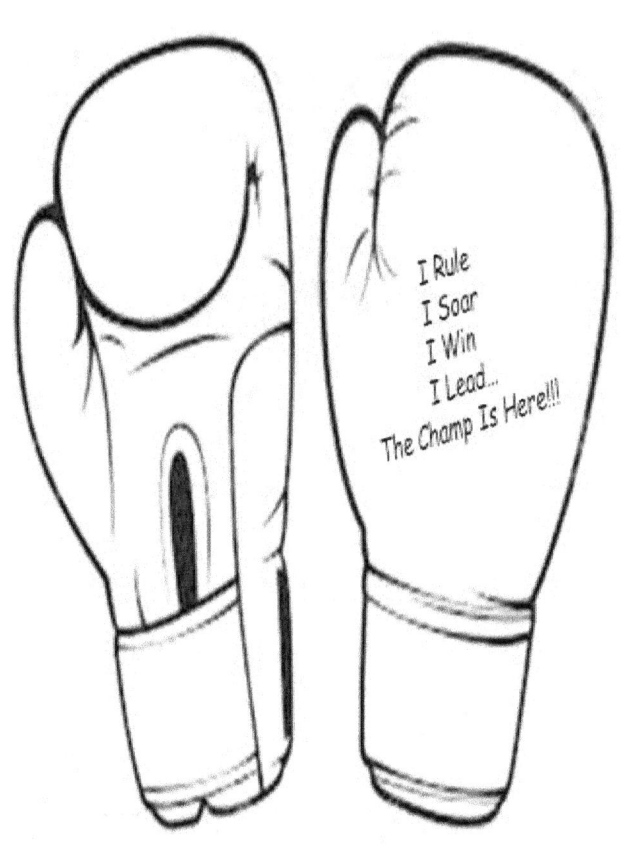

color the gloves in your champion color

I
Accomplish

Logro (Spanish)

How Do You Accomplish?
Cómo se logra (Spanish)

_____
_____
_____
_____

I
Transcend

Yo trasciende (Spanish)

How Do You Transcend?
¿Cómo se trasciende? (Spanish)

_____
_____
_____
_____

I
Transform

Transformar (Spanish)

How Do You Transform?
¿Cómo se transforma? (Spanish)

_____
_____
_____
_____

I
Thrive

Yo prospero (Spanish)

How Do You Thrive?
¿Cómo prosperas? (Spanish)

_____

_____

_____

_____

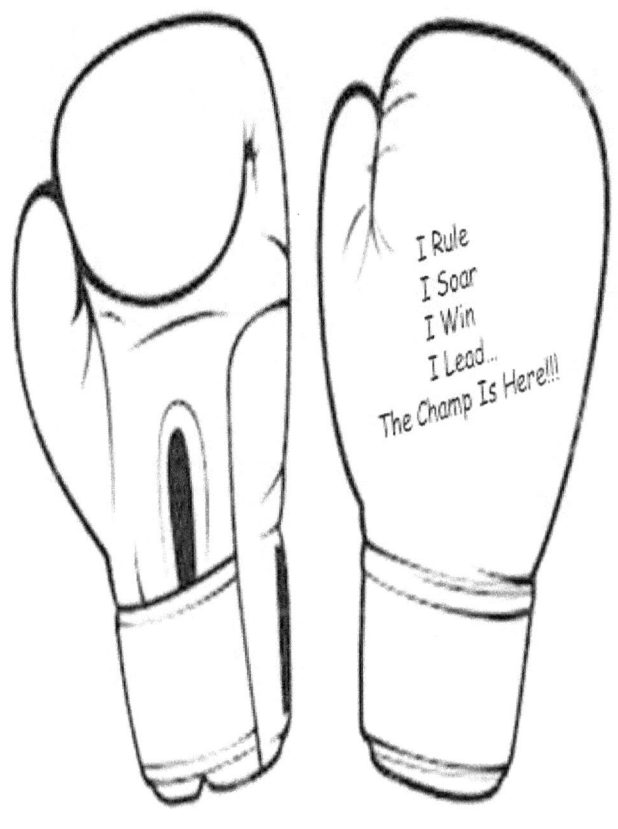

color the gloves in your champion color

I Influence

Yo influyo (Spanish)

How Do You Influence?
¿Cómo influyes? (Spanish)

_____
_____
_____
_____
_____

I Achieve

Lo conseguí (Spanish)

How Do You Achieve?
¿Cómo lo logras? (Spanish)

_____
_____
_____
_____
_____

I Complete

Yo completo (Spanish)

How Do You Complete?
Cómo se completa (Spanish)

_____

_____

_____

_____

_____

I Manage

Yo administro (Spanish)

How Do You Manage?
Cómo te las arreglas (Spanish)

_____
_____
_____
_____
_____

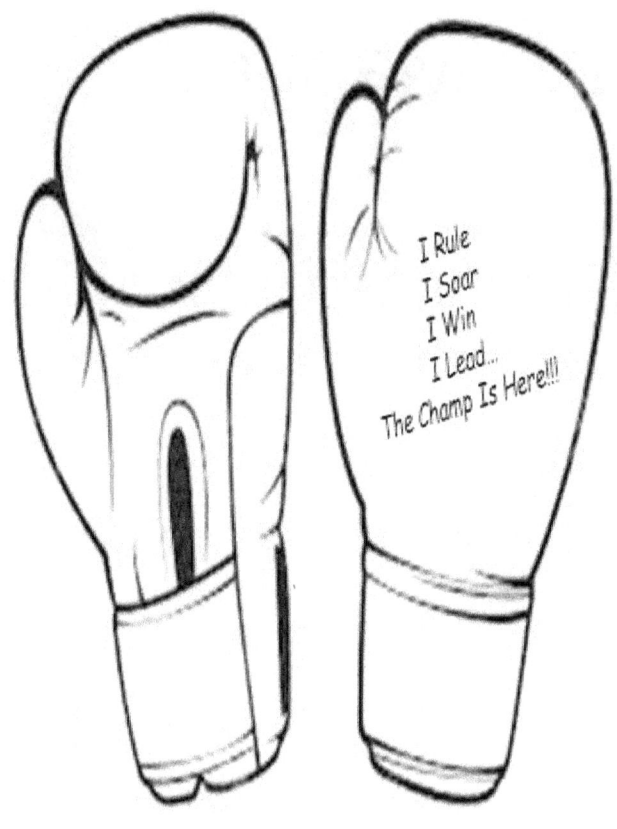

color the gloves in your champion color

I
Win

Yo gano (Spanish)

How Do You Win?
Cómo se gana (Spanish)

_____
_____
_____
_____
_____

I
Rule

Yo mando (Spanish)

How Do You Rule?
¿Cómo gobiernas? (Spanish)

_____
_____
_____
_____
_____

I
Lead

Dirijo (spanish)

How Do You Lead?
Cómo lideras (Spanish)

_____
_____
_____
_____
_____

I
Outlast

I Outlast (same)

How Do You Outlast?
¿Cómo pasas? (Spanish)

_____
_____
_____
_____

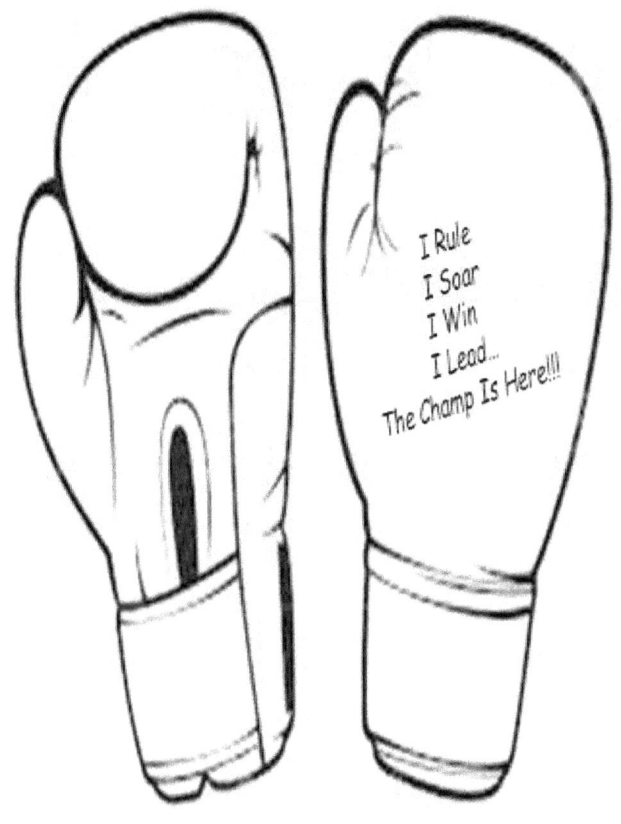

color the gloves in your champion color

I
Outdo

Yo supero (Spanish)

How Do You Outdo?
¿Cómo superas? (Spanish)

_____
_____
_____
_____
_____

I
Out Beat

I Out Beat (same)

How Do You Out Beat?
¿Cómo superas? (Spanish)

_____
_____
_____
_____
_____

I Come Through

Vengo a través (Spanish)

How Do You Come Through?
¿Cómo atraviesas? (Spanish)

_____

_____

_____

_____

_____

I Shine

Yo brillo (Spanish)

How Do You Shine?
¿Cómo brillas? (Spanish)

_____

_____

_____

_____

The Champ Is Here

I
Surpass

Sobrepaso (Spanish)

How Do You Surpass?
¿Cómo superas? (Spanish)

_____
_____
_____
_____
_____

I Dominate

Yo domino (Spanish)

How Do You Dominate?
¿Cómo dominas? (Spanish)

_____

_____

_____

_____

I
Defeat

Derribo (Spanish)

How Do You Defeat?
¿Cómo vences? (Spanish)

_____
_____
_____
_____
_____

I
Out
Smart

Salgo inteligente (Spanish)

How Do You Out Smart?
¿Cómo salgo inteligente? (Spanish)

_____

_____

_____

_____

I
Baffle

I Baffle (same)

How Do You Baffle?
¿Cómo te decepciona? (Spanish)

_____
_____
_____
_____

I
Confuse

Confundo (Spanish)

How Do You Confuse?
¿Cómo confundes? (Spanish)

_____
_____
_____
_____

I
Amaze

Yo asombro (Spanish)

How Do You Amaze?
¿Cómo te sorprende? (Spanish)

_____
_____
_____
_____
_____

The Champ Is Here

Use The Space Provided To Define These Words

Utilice el espacio provisto para definir estas palabras (Spanish)

Determination:

_____

_____

_____

_____

Endurance

_____

_____

_____

Stamina

_____

_____

_____

Perseverance

_____

_____

_____

_____

Excitement

_____

_____

_____

Joy

_____

_____

_____

_____

Accomplish

_____

_____

_____

Attain

_____

_____

_____

_____

Acquire

_____

_____

_____

Engage

_____

_____

_____

_____

Practice

_____

_____

_____

Finish

_____

_____

_____

_____

Create

_____

_____

_____

Perform

_____

_____

_____

_____

Measure Up

_____

_____

_____

Excel

_____

_____

_____

_____

Commit

_____

_____

_____

Out Do

_____

_____

_____

_____

Carry Out

_____

_____

_____

Complete

_____

_____

_____

_____

Realize

_____

_____

_____

Efficacy

_____

_____

_____

Tenacity

_____

_____

_____

Germinate

Kids

Utilize The Next Few Pages And Write Down What You Plan To Do To Stay On The Championship Road

_____

_____

_____

_____

WORD SEARCH

Find These Phrases

I	I	F	I	G	H	T	P	I	I	I	R	Z	O
W	L	E	C	X	E	I	M	E	O	T	I	I	I
I	B	A	T	T	L	E	K	N	U	H	C	D	D
N	E	V	W	O	T	X	E	D	T	R	O	E	O
G	F	C	N	Y	E	C	N	U	D	I	M	E	M
I	L	E	A	D	X	E	I	R	O	V	P	E	I
C	E	N	I	W	I	L	H	E	Q	E	L	A	N
I	C	O	N	F	S	X	S	T	P	U	E	T	A
I	B	A	F	F	L	E	I	U	R	Q	T	E	T
T	H	E	C	H	A	M	P	I	S	H	E	R	E
Q	U	X	A	C	Y	B	Z	C	C	Z	K	U	B
I	A	M	A	Z	E	I	C	O	M	P	E	T	E
I	S	U	R	P	A	S	S	M	I	G	F	X	C
I	O	U	T	L	A	S	T	P	R	O	A	B	T

1. The Champ Is Here
2. I Fight
3. I Win
4. I Battle
5. I Compete
6. I Slay
7. I Conquer
8. I Endure
9. I Excel
10. I Complete
11. I Rule
12. I Lead
13. I Out Last
14. I Out Do
15. I Shine
16. I Surpass
17. I Dominate
18. I Defeat
19. I Baffle
20. I Amaze

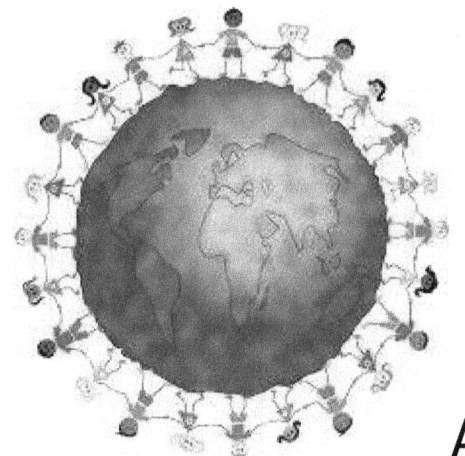

A Special Dedication To ALL THE CHILDREN WITH LOVE In COUNTRIES AROUND THE WORLD

- A

- Afghanistan
- Albania
- Algeria
- Andorra
- Angola
- Antigua and Barbuda
- Argentina
- Armenia
- Australia
- Austria
- Azerbaijan
- B
- Bahamas
- Bahrain
- Bangladesh
- Barbados
- Belarus
- Belgium
- Belize
- Benin
- Bhutan
- Bolivia
- Bosnia and Hiszegovina
- Botswana
- Brazil
- Brunei
- Bulgaria
- Burkina Faso
- Burundi
- C
- Cabo Verde
- Cambodia
- Cameroon
- Canada
- Central African Republic (CAR)
- Chad
- Chile
- China
- Colombia
- Comoros

- Democratic Republic of the Congo
- Republic of the Congo
- Costa Rica
- Cote d'Ivoire
- Croatia
- Cuba
- Cyprus
- Czech Republic
- D
- Denmark
- Djibouti
- Dominica
- Dominican Republic
- E
- Ecuador
- Egypt
- El Salvador
- Equatorial Guinea
- Eritrea
- Estonia
- Ethiopia
- F
- Fiji
- Finland
- France
- G
- Gabon
- Gambia
- Georgia
- Germany
- Ghana
- Greece
- Grenada
- Guatemala
- Guinea
- Guinea-Bissau
- Guyana
- H
- Haiti

- Honduras
- Hungary
- I
- Iceland
- India
- Indonesia
- Iran
- Iraq
- Ireland
- Israel
- Italy
- J
- Jamaica
- Japan
- Jordan
- K
- Kazakhstan
- Kenya
- Kiribati
- Kosovo
- Kuwait
- Kyrgyzstan
- L
- Laos
- Latvia
- Lebanon
- Lesotho
- Liberia
- Libya
- Liechtenstein
- Lithuania
- Luxembourg
- M
- Macedonia
- Madagascar
- Malawi
- Malaysia
- Maldives
- Mali
- Malta
- Marshall Islands
- Mauritania
- Mauritius
- Mexico
- Micronesia
- Moldova
- Monaco
- Mongolia

- Montenegro
- Morocco
- Mozambique
- Myanmar (Burma)
- N
- Namibia
- Nauru
- Nepal
- Netherlands
- New Zealand
- Nicaragua
- Niger
- Nigeria
- North Korea
- Norway
- O
- Oman
- P
- Pakistan
- Palau
- Palestine
- Panama
- Papua New Guinea
- Paraguay
- Peru
- Philippines
- Poland
- Portugal
- Q
- Qatar
- R
- Romania
- Russia
- Rwanda
- S
- St. Kitts and Nevis
- St. Lucia
- St. Vincent and the Grenadines
- Samoa
- San Marino
- Sao Tome and Principe

- Saudi Arabia
- Senegal
- Serbia
- Seychelles
- Sierra Leone
- Singapore
- Slovakia
- Slovenia
- Solomon Islands
- Somalia
- South Africa
- South Korea
- South Sudan
- Spain
- Sri Lanka
- Sudan
- Suriname
- Swaziland
- Sweden
- Switzerland
- Syria
- T
- Taiwan
- Tajikistan
- Tanzania
- Thailand
- Timor-Leste
- Togo
- Tonga
- Trinidad and Tobago
- Tunisia
- Turkey
- Turkmenistan
- Tuvalu
- U
- Uganda
- Ukraine
- United Arab Emirates (UAE)
- United Kingdom (UK)
- United

States of America (USA)
- Uruguay
- Uzbekistan
- V
- Vanuatu
- Vatican City (Holy See)
- Venezuela
- Vietnam
- Y
- Yemen
- Z
- Zambia
- Zimbabwe

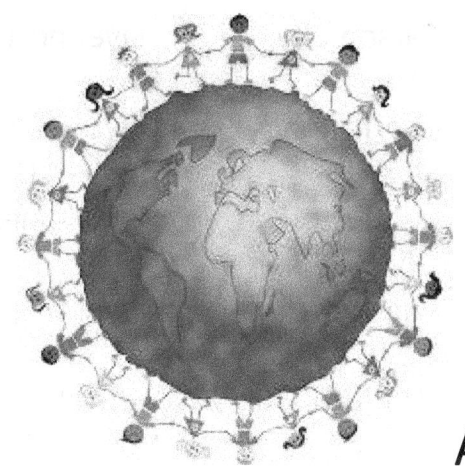

ANOTHER SPECIAL DEDICATION TO ALL THE CHILDREN WITH LOVE IN CITIES IN THE UNITED STATES OF AMERICA

Find Your City And Highlight It

- Albany, NY
- Albuquerque, NM
- Anchorage, AK
- Annapolis, MD
- Atlanta, GA
- Atlantic City, NJ
- Augusta, ME
- Austin, TX
- Bakersfield, CA
- Baltimore, MD
- Baton Rouge, LA
- Billings, MT
- Biloxi, MS
- Bismarck, ND
- Bloomsburg, PA
- Boise, ID
- Boston, MA
- Buffalo, NY
- Burlington, VT
- Carson City, NV
- Charleston, SC
- Charleston, WV
- Charlotte, NC
- Charlottesville, VA
- Cheyenne, WY
- Chicago, IL
- Chicago, IL
- Cleveland, OH
- Colorado Springs, CO
- Columbia, SC
- Columbus, OH
- Concord, CA
- Concord, NH
- Corpus Christi, TX
- Dallas, TX
- Davenport, IA
- Daytona, FL
- Denver, CO
- Des Moines, IA
- Des Plaines, IL
- Detroit, MI
- Dover, DE
- Durham, NC
- Erie, PA
- Eugene, OR
- Fayetteville, NC
- Flagstaff, AZ
- Frankfort, KY
- Ft. Lauderdale, FL
- Gettysburg, PA
- Greenville, SC
- Hampton Roads, VA
- Harrisburg, PA

Hartford, CThroough

Helena, MT
Hollywood, CA
Honolulu, HI
Houston, TX
Huntsville, AL
Indianapolis, IN
Jackson, MS
Jackson Hole-Grand Tetons, WY
Jacksonville, FL
Jefferson City, MO
Jim Thorpe, PA
Juneau, AK
Kansas City, MO
Knoxville, TN
Lake Tahoe, NV

Lancaster, PA
Lancaster / Central PA
Lansing, MI
Las Vegas, NV
Las Vegas, NV
Lexington, KY
Lincoln, NE
Little Rock, AR
Long Island, NY
Los Angeles, CA
Los Angeles, CA
Louisville, KY
Madison, WI
Manchester, NH
Maryville, TN

Memphis, TN
Miami, FL
Miami, FL
Milwaukee, WI
Minneapolis, MN
Mobile, AL
Montgomery, AL
Montpelier, VT
Morrison, IL
Nashville, TN
New Haven, CT
New Orleans, LA
New York: Bronx
New York: Brooklyn
New York: Manhattan
New York: Queens

- New York City
- Newark, NJ
- Niagara Falls, NY
- Northville, MI
- Oklahoma City, OK
- Orlando, FL
- Olympia, WA
- Omaha, NE
- Orange County, CA
- Palm Springs, CA
- Pensacola, FL
- Philadelphia, PA
- Phoenix, AZ
- Pierre, SD
- Pittsburgh, PA
- Portland, ME
- Portland, OR
- Providence, RI
- Pueblo, CO
- Raleigh, NC
- Rapid City, SD
- Reno, NV
- Richmond, VA
- Sacramento, CA
- Salt Lake City, UT
- San Diego, CA
- San Francisco, CA
- Santa Cruz, CA
- Santa Fe, NM
- Scranton, PA
- Seattle, WA
- Sedona, AZ
- Shreveport, LA
- Silicon Valley, CA
- Springfield, IL
- St. Joseph, MO
- St. Paul, MN
- St. Louis, MO
- State College, PA
- SurfScranton, PA
- Syracuse, NY
- Tacoma, WA
- Tallahassee, FL
- Tampa, FL
- Topeka, KS
- Trenton, NJ
- Tulsa, OK
- Tuscon, AZ
- Tyler, TX
- Washington, DC
- Wichita, KS
- Wilkes-Barre, PA

Williamsburg, VA
Williamsport, PA
Wilmington, DE
Yuma, AZ

Thank You

For Purchasing This Book

Pamela Denise Brown

Contact Information
Website:

Booksspeakforyou.com
Pamela Denise Brown Enterprises.com

1-800-757-0598
OR
267-318-8933
@Booksspeakforu (twitter)

Email:
Booksspeakforyou@yahoo.com
FaceBook @Booksspeakforyou

BOOKS SPEAK FOR YOU

www.ingramcontent.com/pod-product-compliance
Lightning Source LLC
Chambersburg PA
CBHW060419050426
42449CB00009B/2033